Peace, Joy, and Happiness to:

Joy

To The World

A Card & More
Mary Lou Brown & Sandy Mahony

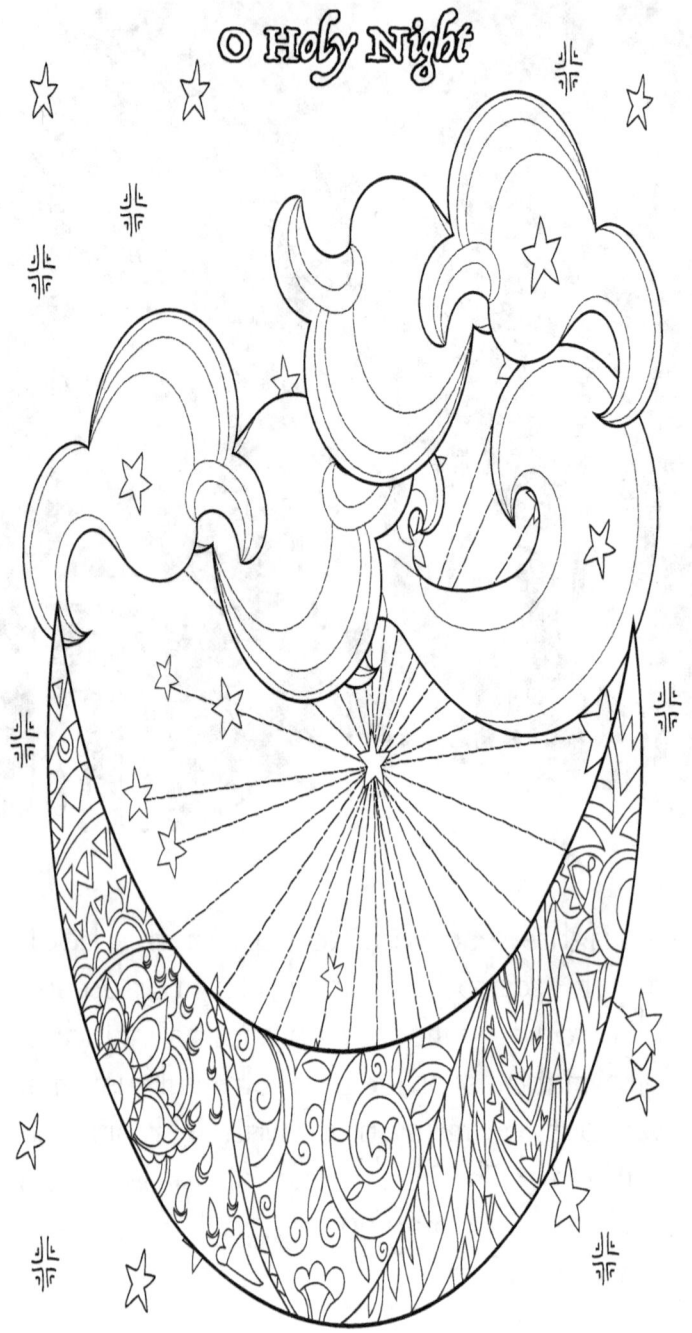

HARK THE HERALD ANGELS SING

Peace
on
Earth

May the closeness of friends,
the comfort of home,
and the
blessings of the birth
of Jesus Christ
renew your spirits this
holiday season.

Star of wonder
Star of light
Guide us to thy
perfect light.

In this
loveliest
of seasons,
let the
spirit of love
gently fill
our hearts
and homes.

For unto us a child is born,
unto us a son is given
and the government
shall be upon his shoulder,
And his name shall be called

Wonderful
Counselor,
Mighty God,
Everlasting
Father,
Prince of
Peace.

Isaiah 9:6

adventurelearningpress.com